GETTING STARTED WITH THE MOTO G

AN INSANELY EASY GUIDE TO THE G FAST, G POWER, G STYLUS, AND G PRO

SCOTT LA COUNTE

RIDICULOUSLY
SIMPLE BOOKS

ANAHEIM, CALIFORNIA

www.RidiculouslySimpleBooks.com

Table of Contents

Disclaimer: *Please note, while every effort has been made to ensure accuracy, this book is not endorsed by Motorola Mobility LLC and should be considered unofficial.*

INTRODUCTION

You've probably been dazzled with commercials for the latest, greatest smartphones. They have features that are supposed to blow your socks offs–and in the process, blow a hole right through your wallet! But not all phones are created alike, and spending a paycheck on a device smaller than some hands isn't always required. There are budget devices that pack power into a much smaller price point.

The Moto G is a fast, powerful, and feature packed phone that will have you bragging to friends about how much money you saved buying a phone for a fraction of the price of other phones. It has an impressive camera, plenty of RAM, and supports all the apps you love. It may not have multiple camera lenses, but for a lot of people that's not exactly important.

If you have a Moto G and want to make sure you understand all the popular features, this guide can help you out. It covers:

- Setting up your phone
- Making calls
- Installing apps
- Using the camera
- Surfing the Internet
- Changing system settings

And much more!

Are you ready to get started?!

[1]

START HERE

This chapter will cover:
- What's new
- Cosmetics of the phone
- How does it compare

SETTING UP THE PHONE

You have a new phone. I know your excited to turn it on and start using it. But it's not like a TV. You don't just plug it in and power it on. You must go through a setup first.

Here's the good news: it's easy. So easy that you can actually skip this part of the book and just follow the instructions.

I'm going to breeze through the setup and quickly walk you through what some of the screens are and why it's asking you, but I will point out here that there are several Moto G devices. So my setup might look a *little* different from yours—that's especially true if your phone has Android 12 and not 11 (I'll explain that in the next section).

When you power it on, the first thing you'll see is a "Hi there" screen with a Start button in yellow. If you need anything larger, you can go to the bottom right corner to Vision settings.

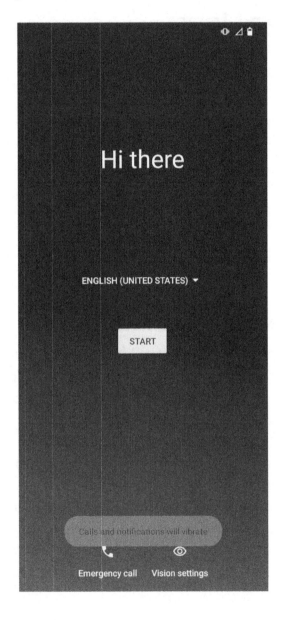

Next, you'll see a screen to setup wi-fi, and then a Getting your phone ready screen. You'll see a lot of those screens throughout the setup. You'll probably see it spinning for over a minute. That's fine. Just be patient.

Getting your phone ready...
This may take a few minutes

After it's "ready" it's going to present you with legal docs that you need to agree to. You can either spend the evening reading through them or be like most people and tap accept. You can also adjust the toggles to turn on and off different privacy settings.

Privacy & software updates

Motorola collects and reports usage information
to keep your software up to date, provide
personalized support, and improve products and
services. You can change your privacy preferences
anytime by going to Settings > Privacy > Motorola
privacy.

Help improve Motorola products
Share device usage statistics.

Enhanced device support
Get customized support and recommendations for
your device.

Smart updates
Automatically download & install security updates
and bug fixes over Wi-Fi.

For your safety, security updates may download & install
automatically over mobile data if Wi-Fi isn't available within a
timeframe that corresponds to the importance of the update.
Critical updates may also download & install automatically
over Wi-Fi if they're needed to keep your device working
properly.

Motorola privacy policy

Screenshot saved   Accept & continue

‹

If you have another device, you can copy over all the settings (like apps and contacts) in the next section. Or you can select "Don't copy" in the lower left corner.

Copy apps & data

You can choose to transfer your apps, photos,
contacts, Google Account, and more.

Don't copy

Next

<

Android is a Google operating system, so they love you to have a Google account. That syncs all their products nicely with the phone. If you don't have an account, you can create one right here—if you do, then you can sign into it. If you don't want to take advantages of using Google free services or Gmail on the phone, then you can select Skip in the lower left corner.

Google

Sign in

with your Google Account. Learn more

Email or phone

Forgot email?

Create account

Skip

Next

‹

Once you add your account, you get more terms you have to agree to.

We publish the Google Terms of Service so that you know what to expect as you use our services. By clicking 'I Agree,' you agree to these terms.

You are also agreeing to the Google Play Terms of Service to enable discovery and management of apps.

And remember, the Google Privacy Policy describes how Google handles information generated as you use Google services. You can always visit your Google Account (account.google.com) to take a Privacy Checkup or to adjust your privacy controls.

Don't add this account now

I agree

Next is another gathering info type screen. Again, this might take several minutes to complete. Don't worry if it's been more than a minute of spinning.

Getting account info...

Once it's done, there's several Google Services you can opt in or out of. These are free, but do take data—which might not be free on your carrier plan.

Google Services

roboscott@gmail.com
Tap to learn more about each service, such as how
to turn it on or off later. Data will be used according
to Google's Privacy Policy.

Backup & storage

Back up to Google Drive ∨

Easily restore your data or switch
devices at any time. Your backup
includes apps, app data, call history,
contacts, device settings (including
Wi-Fi passwords and permissions),
and SMS.

Your backups are securely encrypted
and uploaded to Google. For some
data, your device's screen lock PIN,
pattern or password is used for
enhanced protection.

Location

Use location ∨

Allow apps and services with
location permission to use your
device's location. Google may collect
location data periodically and use
this data in an anonymous way

More

‹

From here, there's a password protect setup screen.
This is so when you turn on your phone after it's been on
standby, you'll need to put in a code. It's helpful if you
lose your phone, so your info stays protected. It's also
optional, so you can skip it in the lower left corner.

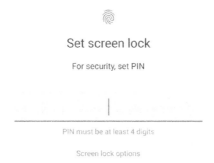

At this point, there's a few more things to setup, but if you are super antsy about using the phone, then you can skip it. There's just a few more minutes left, so I recommend continuing. If you don't continue, you can go back and change them later.

Continue setup?

Keep going to get your phone fully set up. Or, leave
now and get a reminder to finish later.

If you tap continue, you'll see another loading screen.
Again, prepare to wait.

Just a sec...

Your Assistant will be right with you

The first screen is for Google Assistant. This is so you can ask your phone to do things by voice. So, you can say something like "Hey Google call my mom." And it will start dialing her.

Access your Assistant with "Hey Google"

Say "Hey Google" to get hands free help
from the Google Assistant. By allowing
this, your phone will wait for you to say
"Hey Google".

Do it later   Yes, I'm in

‹

Next, you'll get a list of several other options to adjust.

The next screen is to get offers and text from Moto; by default, it's toggled on. Don't want them? Just tap the toggle switches to turn them off.

Let's stay in touch

Personalize your experience
Learn about features that are important to you.

Be the first to know
Get information about software updates and
new products.

Be heard
Receive invitations to participate in studies
and surveys.

Get exclusive access
Take advantage of special offers.

Subscribe for emails

The final steps is to get a quick tutorial of how the
phone works. Just tap next until the last screen.

Go home

To go to the Home screen, swipe up from the
bottom of the screen

Next

‹

Finally, the last screen. It has no buttons to continue. That's because you are supposed to practice the swipe up gesture. Once you swipe up, you'll be done.

Give it a try

Swipe up to go to the Home screen. You can
manage your navigation preferences in Settings

Go to Settings

WHAT'S NEW IN ANDROID 11

Before we get started, let's talk OS. This will be one of more confusing things in this book.

OS stands for operating system. It's how your phone looks and acts. Windows 95? That's an operating system. All phones have them. In the case of Moto G, the OS is Android.

Not too complicated yet, right?

Here's the problem with Android. Every year Google, who makes Android, releases a new version. In 2021, they released Android 12. The problem is it's up to the manufacture to make the update available to the phone.

So, what does all that mean? Chances are, your phone does not have Android 12 yet—unless you bought this book a few months after the publication date. More than likely, it has Android 11 (though some might even have Android 10). I'll walk you through updating the OS later, but that's not an option until Motorola pushes it out.

Here's the good news: OS updates with Android are not typically major. A few new features are added in and the "look" will change slightly. But you should still know how to use the phone and where to find things.

WHAT A DIFFERENCE A PHONE MAKES

The Moto G lineup mostly differs in price; the features tend to be more minor. The biggest difference between the Moto G Stylus and Moto G power, for example, is the Moto G Stylus comes with...you guessed it, a stylus! The Moto G Fast is cheaper, but the specs are still very good. The resolution isn't as great, and the front camera is 8MP (vs 16MP on the more expensive phones), but the back camera is essentially the same. They all shoot 4K video as well. The Stylus and Power both have 4GB of RAM (the Fast has 3GB); the memory on each phone also varies--the stylus has the most.

Those specs come pretty close to what you will get on the budget Samsung Galaxy A33 and iPhone SE.

FINDING YOUR WAY AROUND

People come to the Moto G from all sorts of different places: iPhone, other Android phone, flip phone, two styrofoam cups tied together with string. This next section is a crash course in the interface. If you've used Android before, then it might seem a little simple, so skip ahead if you already know all of this.

If any of this seems a little rushed, there's good reason: it is! We'll cover these points in more detail later. This is just a quick starter / reference.

On the bottom of your screen is the shortcut bar—you'll be spending a lot of time here; you can add whatever you want to this area, but these are the apps Google thinks you'll use most—and, with the exception of the Play Store, they are probably right.

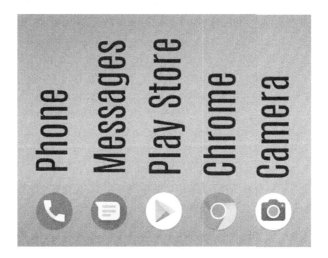

So, what are these? Real quick, these are as follows:

- **Phone**: Do you want to take a wild guess what the phone button does? If you said brings you an ice cream, then maybe you aren't cut out for a phone. But if you said something along the lines of "It launches an app to call people" then you'll have no problem at all with your new device. Surprise, surprise: this pricey gadget that plays games, takes pictures, and keeps you up to date on political ramblings on social media does one more interesting thing: it calls people!
- **Message**: Message might be a little more open-ended than "Phone"; that could mean email message, text messages, messages you keep getting on your bathroom mirror to put the toilet seat down. In this case, it means "text messages" (but really—put that toilet seat down...you aren't doing anyone any favors). This is the app you'll use whenever you want to text cute pictures of cats.
- **Play Store**: Anything with the word "Play" in the title must be fun, right?! This app is what you'll use to download all those fun apps you always hear about.

- **Chrome**: Whenever you want to surf the Internet, you'll use Chrome. There are actually several apps that do the same thing—like Firefox and Opera—but I recommend Chrome until you are comfortable with your phone. Personally, I think it's the best app for searching the Internet, but you'll soon learn that most things on the phone are about preference, and you may find another Internet browser that suits your needs more.
- **Camera**: This apps opens pictures of vintage cameras...just kidding! It's how you take pictures on your phone. You use this same app for videos as well.

Next to the shortcut bar, the area you'll use the most is the notification bar. This is where you'll get, you guessed it, notifications! What's a notification? That's any kind of notice you have elected to receive. A few examples: text message alerts, email alerts, amber alerts, and apps that have updates.

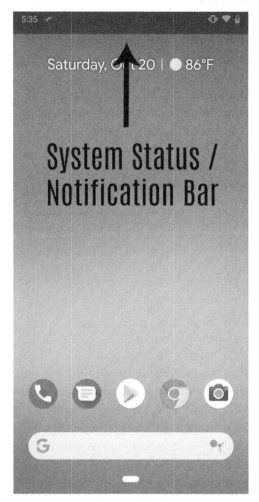

When you drag your finger down from the notification bar, you'll get a list of several settings that you can adjust. Press and hold any of these options and you'll open an app with even more options.

From right to left these are the options you can change or use:

- Wi-fi
- Bluetooth
- Do not disturb
- Flashlight
- Lock the device from auto-rotating
- Turn on / off battery saving

If you continue dragging down, this thin menu expands and there are a few more options—four to be exact.

The first is at the top of the screen—it's the slider, and it makes your device brighter or dimmer depending on which way you drag it. You can slide your finger to see more options:

- **Data** – Tapping this turns your data on and off, which is handy if you are running low on data and don't want to be charged extra for it.
- **Airplane mode** - This turns off Bluetooth, data, and wi-fi and makes your device ready to use on an airplane.
- **Night light** - This is a special mode that dims your screen and makes the screen appropriate for reading in dark settings.
- **Battery share** – when you press this, you can use your device like a wireless charger. What does that mean? Let's say your friend has an iPhone with wireless charging and they're almost out of battery. You can press this, then hold their phone against yours and share your battery wirelessly with them.
- **Screen Record** – Screen recording used to be something you needed a special app for; Android 11 brings native recording. So you can record

what you are doing on your screen and share it with someone else. It's great for tutorial videos. You are also able to use your phone's microphone to narrate with your voice.

Something else that's pretty cool on this notification area: you can see a history of notifications.

If you get a lot of notifications, you probably have accidentally dismissed something that you didn't mean to. Now you can see what it was.

To use it, go to the bottom of all your notifications, then select "Manage."

From here, toggle "Use notification history" to on.

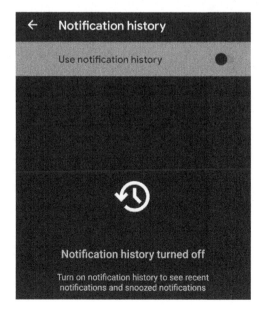

Now when you go back to that same area "Manage" is replaced with "History."

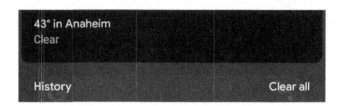

FEELING HOME-LESS?

You may have noticed something that seems important missing from your phone: a Home button. On older phones, this was a critical button that gets you to the Home screen whenever you push it.

How on Earth do you get Home without a Home button?! Easy. Are you ready? Swipe up. That's it!

If you've used any Apple device, then you might know a thing or two about Siri. She's the assistant that "sometimes" works; Google has its own version of Siri and it's called Google Assistant. The names not quite as creative as Siri, but many say it works better. I'll let you be the judge of that.

To get to the Google Assistant from anywhere, just say "Ok, Google." If you are on the Home screen, then there's also a Google Assistant widget. This little bar does more than make appointments and get your information—it's also a global search. What does that mean? It means you can type in anything you want to know, and it will search both the Internet and your phone. If it's a contact in your phone, then it will get you that. But if it's the opening hours for the Museum of Strange then it will search the Internet—it will also give you a map of the location and the phone number.

GET AROUND ON YOUR MOTO G PHONE

When it comes to getting around your Moto G, learning how to use gestures will be the quickest, most effective method. You can change some of the gesture options by going to the Settings app, then System > Gestures > System navigation.

The most important gesture is how to get back to the Home screen—there are no buttons after all. That's the easiest one to remember: swipe up from the bottom of the screen.

When you are on an Internet page, you can swipe from the left or right edge of the screen to go backwards or forwards.

To select text, tap and hold over the text, then lift your finger when it responds.

MULTITASKING

Those are the easy gestures to remember; if you want to move around quickly, however, you need to know the two big multitask gestures, which help you switch between apps.

The first is to see your open apps. To do this, swipe up like you're going to the Home screen, but keep going until about the middle of the screen and then stop and lift your finger—don't make a quick swipe-up gesture like you would when going Home. This will show you previews of all of your open apps, and you can swipe between them. Tap the one you want to open.

The quickest way to switch back and forth between two or three apps, however, is to swipe from left to right along the bottom edge of the screen. This swipes between apps in the order that you have used them.

ZOOM

Need to see text bigger? There are two ways to do that. Note: this works on many, but not all apps.

The first way is to pinch to zoom.

r with the Additic
: between you an
es. It is importan
Collectively, this l
s".

etween what the
al Terms say, ther
elation to that Se

The second way is to double tap on the text.

ROTATE

You probably have noticed if you rotate your phone, it rotates the screen. What if you don't want to rotate the entire screen? You can turn that off very easily. Swipe down and then tap the "arrows" button to enable or disable it.

[3]

THE RIDICULOUSLY SIMPLE OVERVIEW OF ALL THE THINGS YOU SHOULD KNOW

This chapter will cover:
- Customizing screens
- Split screens
- Gestures

MAKING PRETTY SCREENS

If you've used an iPhone or iPad, then you may notice the screen looks a little...bare. There's literally nothing on it. Maybe you like that. If so, then good for you! Skip ahead. If you want to decorate that screen with shortcuts and widgets, then read on.

ADDING SHORTCUTS

Any app you want on this screen, just find it, and then press and hold; when a menu comes up, drag it upward until the screen appears and move it to where you want it to go. You can also drag it to new screens.

To remove an app from a screen, tap and hold, then drag it upward to the "Remove" text that appears when you move it up. When it's there, let go.

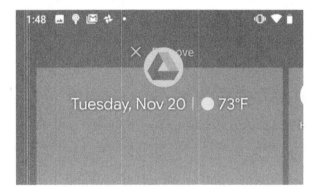

Widgets

Shortcuts are nice, but widgets are better. Widgets are sort of like mini-programs that run on your screen. A common widget people put on their screen is the weather forecast. Throughout the day the widget will update automatically with up-to-date info.

To add a widget, go to the screen you want to add it to and tap and hold until the menu comes up.

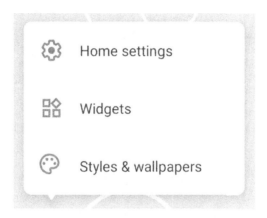

Select "Widgets." This opens up a widget library—it's like a mini app store.

When you find one you want to add, tap and hold it, then drag it to the screen you want to add it to.

Widgets come in all sorts of shapes and sizes, but most of them can be resized. To resize it, tap and hold it. If you see little circles, then you can tap those and drag it in or out to make it bigger or smaller.

You remove widgets the same way you remove shortcuts. Tap and hold and then drag it upward to the remove.

WALLPAPER

Adding wallpaper to your screen is done in a similar way. Tap and hold your finger on the Home screen, when the menu comes up, select "Wallpaper" instead of "Widgets." Some of the options even move—so the wallpaper always has something moving across your screen—it's like a slow moving movie.

Wallpapers

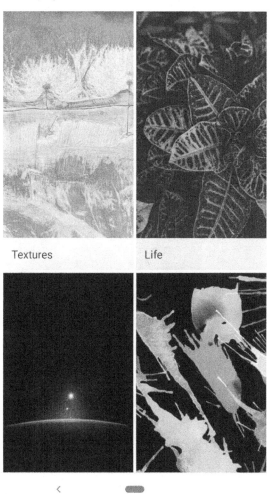

When you have a wallpaper open that you want to add, just hit the "Set Wallpaper" in the upper right corner.

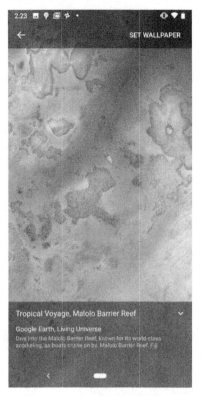

STYLES

Picking wallpaper for your phone helps give it a bit more personality, but Style helps really finetune the customization. You can pick icon shapes, fonts, and more.

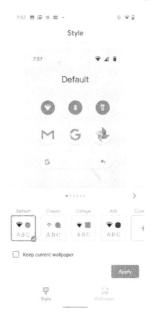

To use it, go to Settings > Display > Styles; make sure and tap "Apply" when you finish up.

A WORD, OR TWO, ABOUT MENUS

It's pretty intuitive that if you tap on an icon, it opens the app. What's not so obvious is if you tap and hold there are other options. Every app is different. Usually, they're shortcuts—tapping and holding over the Phone icon, for example, brings up your favorites; doing the same thing over the camera brings up a selfie mode shortcut. Tap and hold over your favorite apps to see what shortcuts are available.

SPIT SCREENS

The Moto G phone comes in two different sizes; the bigger screen obviously gives you a lot more space, which makes split screen apps a pretty handy feature. It works on the smaller Moto G as well, though it doesn't feel as effective on the smaller screen.

To use this feature, swipe up to bring up multitasking; next, tap the icon above the window you want to turn into split screen (note:

this feature is not supported on all apps); if split screen is available, you'll see a menu that has an option for split screen.

Once you tap "split screen," it will let you swipe left and right to find the app you want to split the screen with. Tap the one you want.

Your screen is now split in two.

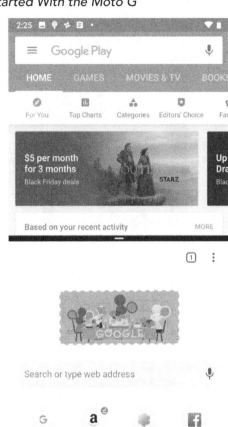

That thin black bar in the middle is adjustable; you can move it up or down so one of the apps has more screen real estate.

To exit this mode, drag the black bar either all the way to the top or all the way to the bottom until one of the apps completely goes away.

GESTURES

JUMP TO CAMERA

Press the power button twice to quickly jump to the camera.

DOUBLE-TAP

If your phone is in standby, double-tap the screen and the time and notifications will appear.

GOOGLE ASSISTANT

Google Assistant can be trigged by saying "Hey, Google". With gestures, there's a new way: swipe from either the right or left bottom corner.

Hi, how can I help?

[4]

THE BASICS…AND KEEP IT RIDICULOUSLY SIMPLE

This chapter will cover:
- Making calls
- Sending messages
- Finding and downloading apps
- Driving directions

Now that you have your phone set up and know your way around the device at its most basic level, let's go over the apps you'll be using the most that are currently on your shortcut or favorite bar:
- Phone
- Messages
- Google Play Store
- Chrome

Notice that Camera is off this list? There's a lot to cover with Camera, so I'll go over it in a separate chapter.

Before we get into it, there's something you need to know: how to open apps not on your favorite bar. It's easy. From your home screen, swipe up from the bottom. Notice that menu that's appearing? That's where all the additional apps are.

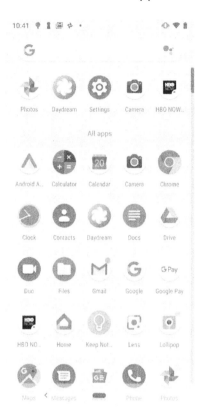

MAKING CALLS

So...who you going to call? Ghostbusters?!

You would be the most awesome person in the world if Ghostbusters was in your phone contacts! But before you can find that number in your contacts, it would probably help to know how to add a contact, find a contact, edit a contact, and put contacts into groups, right? So before we get to making calls, let's do baby steps and cover Contacts.

CONTACTS

So, let's open up the Contacts app to get started. See it? Not on your favorite bar, right? So where is it?! That's why I showed you earlier how to get to additional apps. Swipe up from the bottom of your screen and keep swiping until the menu appears in its entirety.

It's in alphabetical order, so the Contacts app is in the C's. It looks like this:

Contacts

Chances are if you've added your email account, you'll already have a lot of contacts listed. Like hundreds!

You can either scroll slowly, or head to the right-hand side of the app and scroll—this lets you quickly scroll by letters. Just slide your finger until you see the letter of the contact you want and then stop.

I'm getting ahead of myself, however! Before you can scroll, it would be nice to know how to add a contact so there are people to scroll to. To add a contact, tap on that blue plus sign.

Adding a person looks more like applying for a job than adding a contact. There are rows and rows of fields!

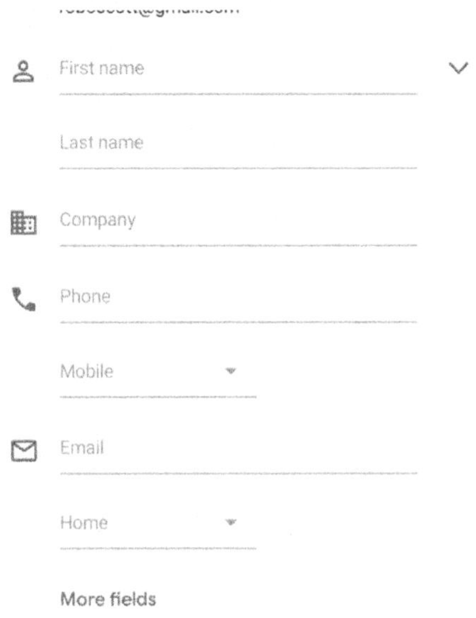

First name ⌄

Last name

Company

Phone

Mobile ▾

Email

Home ▾

More fields

Just in case you weren't overwhelmed by all the fields, you can tap more fields and get even more!

10:43

X   Create contact   ✓   ⋮

AIM   ▾

🌐 Website

📅 Date   ▾

Birthday   ▾

☺ Relationship

Assistant   ▾

📞 SIP

≡ Notes

▭ Label   ▾

☰ Custom field

Custom label

Is that not enough? Google has you covered because you can add a custom field!

Here's the most important thing you need to know: fields are optional! You can add a name and email and that's it. You don't even have to add their phone number. If you want to call them, then that would certainly help though.

If you have a hard time remembering who people are, then you can also take a picture or add a picture you already have. Comes in handy if you have eight kids and you can't remember if Joey is the one with blonde hair or red hair.

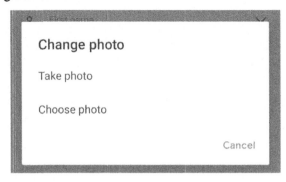

Once you are done, tap the checkbox. That saves it. If you decide you don't want to add a contact after all, the tap the X. That closes it without saving.

EDITING A CONTACT

If you add an email and then later decide you should add a phone number, or if you want to edit anything else, then just find the name in your contacts and tap it once. This brings up all the info you've already added.

Go to the lower corner and tap on the pencil button. This makes the contact editable. Go to your desired field and update. When you are finished, tap the checkbox in the upper right corner.

SHARING A CONTACT

If you have your phone long enough, someone will ask you for so and so's phone number. The old-fashioned way was to write it down. But you have a smartphone, so you aren't old-fashioned!

The new way to share a number is to find the person in your contacts, tap their name, then tap those three dots in the upper right corner of your screen. This brings up a menu.

Delete

Share

Add to Home screen

Set ringtone

Route to voicemail

Help & feedback

There are a few options here, but the one you want is "Share"; from here you have a few options, but the easiest is to text or email the contact to your friend. This sends them a contact card. So if you have other information with that contact (such as email) then that will be sent over as well.

DELETE CONTACT

There are a few more options on that menu I just showed. If you decide a person is dead to you and you never want to contact them again, then you can return to that menu and tap "Delete." This erases them from your phone, but not your life.

GET ORGANIZED

Once you start getting lots of contacts, then it's going to make finding someone more time-consuming. Labels helps. You can add a label for "Family" for instance, and then stick all of your family members there.

When you open your contacts and tap those three lines in the upper left corner, you'll see a menu. This is where you'll see your labels. So with labels, you can jump right into that list and find the contact you need.

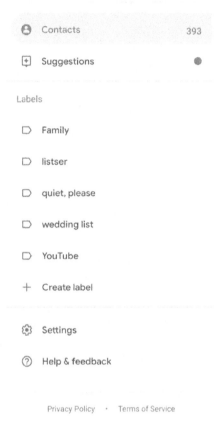

You can also send the entire group inside the label an email or text message. So for instance, if your child is turning 2 and you want to remind everyone in your "Family" contact not to come, then just tap on that label, and then tap on the three dots in the upper right corner. This brings up a menu of options.

Send email

Send message

Remove contacts

Rename label

Delete label

From here, just tap send email or send message.

But what if you don't have labels? Or if you want to add people to a label? Easy. Remember that long application you used to add a contact? One of the fields was called "Labels." You have to tap more to see it. It's all the way at the bottom. One of the last fields, in fact.

If you've never added a label or want to add a new one, then just start typing. If you have another one that you'd like to use, then just tap the arrow and select it.

When you are done, don't forget to tap "Save."

Delete Label

If you decide you no longer want to have a label, then just go to the menu I showed you above—side menu, then the three dots. From here, tap the "Delete Label."

If there's just one person you want to boot from the label, then tap them and go to the label and delete it.

MAKING CALLS

That concludes our sidetrack into the Contacts app. We can now return to getting back to making phone calls to the Ghostbusters.

You can make a call by opening the Contacts app, then selecting the contact, and then tapping on their phone number. Alternatively, you can tap on the Phone button from your Home screen or favorite bar.

There are a few options when you open this app. Let's talk about each one.

Starting from the far left is the Favorites tab. If you tap this, then you'll see your favorite contacts. If you haven't added any, then this will be empty. If you want to make someone your favorite, then tap them in your Contacts, and tap the star on the top by their name. Once you do that, they'll automatically start showing up here.

In the middle is the Recents tab. If you've made any calls, they'll show here.

The last option is Contacts, which opens a version of the Contacts app that's within the Phone app.

Also on the right is the dial button.

If you want to dial someone the old-fashioned way by tapping in numbers, then tap this.

1 ∞	2 ABC	3 DEF
4 GHI	5 JKL	6 MNO
7 PQRS	8 TUV	9 WXYZ
∗	0 +	#

When you are done with the call, hit the "End" button on your phone.

ANSWER AND DECLINE CALLS

What do you do when someone calls you? Probably ignore it because it's a telemarketer!

It's easy to accept a call, however. When the phone rings, the number will appear and if the person is in your Contacts, then the name will appear as well. To answer, just swipe the "answer." To decline just drag the "decline."

Play Angry Birds While Talking to Angry Mom

What if you're on a call with your mom and she's just complaining about something, but you don't want to be rude and hang up? Easy. You multitask! This means you could play Angry Birds while talking!

To multitask, just swipe up from the bottom of your phone, and open the app you want to work in while you are talking. The call will show in the notification area. Tap it to return to the call.

MESSAGES

Now that you know how Contacts and Phone works, messaging will be like second nature. They share many of the same properties. Let's open up the Messages app (it's on your Favorites bar).

Create / Send a Message

When you have selected the contact(s) to send a message to, tap Compose. You can also manually type in the number in the text field.

You can add more than one contact--this is known as a group text.

Use the text field to type out your message. If you want to add anything fancy to your message (like photos or gifs) then tap the plus sign. This brings up a menu with more options.

When you are ready to send your message, tap the arrow with the SMS under it.

VIEW MESSAGE

When you get a message, your phone will vibrate, chirp, or do nothing—it all depends on how you set up your phone. To view the message, you can either open the app, or swipe down to see your notifications—one will be the text message.

CONVERSATIONS

Google took big strides in Android 11 to make replying to messages more streamlined and effortless.

One place you see this is with Conversations. When you get a message (text, Facebook message, Twitter message, etc), you'll see that in your notification area by swiping down from the top.

The old method was to click that message to reply. Now you can see the message, set the priority level, and reply right from this area.

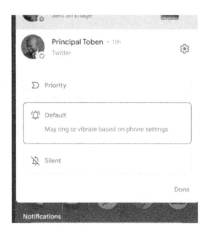

CHAT BUBBLES

Another area you'll see Android 11 streamline approach to messages is with Chat Bubbles. Chat Bubbles will appear on the side of whatever app you are working in, so you can reply without actually closing the app. As the name suggests, they'll be little bubbles on the side of your screen.

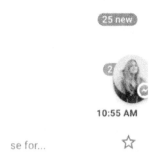

If you aren't crazy about this feature, you can toggle it off by going to the Settings app, then Apps & Notifications> Notifications > Bubbles.

SMART REPLY

If you're a Gmail user, you've probably started to see Smart Replies in your email. Smart Reply uses a computer engine to recognize what you will type next and make a suggestion.

Smart Reply works so surprisingly well you might be a little creeped out by it—like it will feel like some person is on the other end of the screen reading your messages! That's not the case. It's all artificial intelligence. But if you still find the feature either creepy or annoying then you can go to the Settings app, then search for Smart Reply. Under Suggestions in chat, you'll see a on / off toggle for the feature.

WHERE'S AN APP FOR THAT?

I mentioned earlier that you could play Angry Birds while talking to your angry mom on the phone. Sound fun? But where is Angry Birds on your phone? It's not! You have to download it.

Adding and removing apps on the Moto G is easy. Head to your favorite bar on the bottom of your Home screen and tap the Google Play app.

This launches the Play Store.

From here you can browse the top apps, see editors' picks, look through categories, or, if you have an app in mind, search for it. The Play Store isn't just for apps. You can use the tabs on the top to go to movies, books, and music. Any kind of downloadable content that's offered by Google can be found here.

When you see the app you want, tap on it. You can read through reviews, see screenshots, and install it on your phone. To install, simply tap the install button—if it's a paid app you'll be prompted to buy it. If there's no price, it's free (or offers in-app payments—which means the app is free, but there are premium features inside it you may have to pay for).

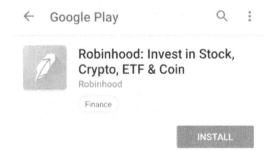

The app is now stored in the app section of your device (remember the section you get to when you swipe up from the bottom to the top?).

REMOVE APP

If you decide you no longer want an app, go to the app in the app menu and tap and hold it. This brings up a box that says "App info." Tap that.

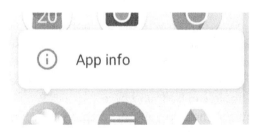

From this menu, you'll get all the information about the app; one of the options is to remove it. Tap that and you're done.

Uninstall		Force stop

Notifications
On

Permissions
No permissions granted

Storage
153 MB used in internal storage

Data usage
82.75 MB used since Oct 25

Advanced
Time spent in app, Battery, Open by default, Sto...

If you download the app from the Play Store, you can always delete it. Some apps that were pre-installed on your phone cannot be deleted.

DRIVING DIRECTIONS

Back in the day, you may have had a GPS. It was a fancy plastic device that would give you directions for anywhere in North America. You can throw out that device because your phone is your new GPS.

To get directions, swipe up to open up your apps. Tap the Maps app.

Maps

It's automatically going to be set to wherever you are currently at—which is both creepy and useful.

To get started, just type where you want to go. I'm searching for Disneyland, Anaheim.

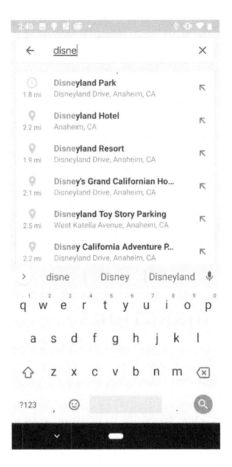

It automatically starts filling in what it thinks you are going to type and tells you the distance. When you see the one you want, tap it.

It pinpoints the location on the map and also gives you an option to call, share or get directions to the location. If you want to zoom out or in, just use two fingers and pinch in or out on the screen.

It automatically gets directions from where you are. Want it from a different location? Just tap on the "Your location" field and type where you want to go. You can also reverse the directions by tapping on the double arrows. When you are ready to go, tap "Start."

What if you don't want to drive? What if you want to walk? Or bike? Or take a taxi? There are options for all of those and more! Tap the slider under the address bar to whatever you prefer. This updates the directions—when you walk, for example, it will show you one-way streets and also update the time it will take you.

What if you want to drive but are like me: terrified of freeways in California? There's an option to avoid highways. Tap the menu button in the upper right corner of the screen, then select what you want to avoid, and hit "done." You are now rerouted to a longer route—notice how the times probably changed?

Options

☐   Avoid highways

☐   Avoid tolls

☐   Avoid ferries

CANCEL   DONE

Once you get your directions, you can swipe up to get turn-by-turn directions. You can even see what it looks like from the street. It's called Street View.

Street View isn't only for streets. Google is expanding the feature everywhere. If you hold your finger over the map, there will be an option to show Street View if it's available. Just tap the thumbnail. Here's a Street View of Disneyland:

You can wander around the entire park! If only you could ride the rides, too! You can get even closer to the action by picking up the Dreamview headset. When you stick your phone in that, you can turn your head and the view turns with you.

Street View is also available in a lot of malls and other tourist attractions. Point your map to the Smithsonian in Washington, DC and get a pretty cool Street View.

SHARING WI-FI

Anytime you have guests over, you almost always get the question: what's your wi-fi password. If you are like me, then it probably annoys you. Maybe your password is really long, maybe you just don't like giving out your password, or maybe you are just too embarrassed to say that it's "Feet$FetishLover1." Whatever the reason, then you will love sharing your wi-fi with QR codes. Gone are the days of giving this info out. Just give them a code that they scan, and they'll have access without ever knowing what your password is.

To use it, go to your wi-fi settings, then select the configure button for the wi-fi you want to share.

This will bring up your wi-fl info; tap the blue "Share" option with the QR code.

Jereiiiaii 29.11

Connected

Forget   Share

Signal strength
Good

Frequency
2.4 GHz

Security
WPA2-Personal

Advanced
Network usage, Privacy, Add device, Network d..

Once you verify that it's you, then you will see the code to scan and you just have to show it to your friend.

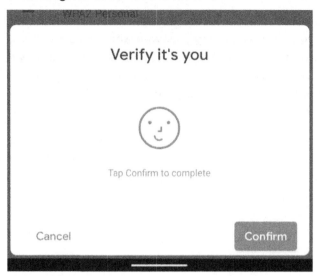

Verify it's you

Tap Confirm to complete

Cancel   Confirm

[5]

LET'S GO SURFING NOW!

This chapter will cover:
- Setting up email
- Creating and sending email
- Managing multiple accounts
- Browsing the Internet

When it comes to the Internet, there are two things you'll want to do:
- Send email
- Browse the Internet

ADD AN EMAIL ACCOUNT

When you set up your phone, you'll set it up to your Google Account, which is usually your email.

You may, however, want to add another email account—or remove the one you set up.

To add an email, swipe up to bring up your apps, and tap on "Settings."

Next, tap on "Accounts."

From here, select "Add Account"; you can also tap on the account that's been set up and tap remove account—but remember you can have more than one account on your phone.

Once you add your email, you'll be asked what type of email it is. Follow the steps after you select the email type to add in your email, password, and other required fields.

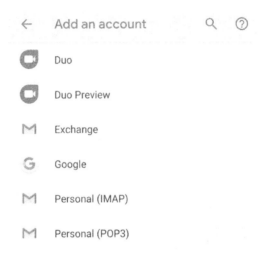

CREATE AND SEND AN EMAIL

To send an email using Gmail (Moto G's native email app), swipe up to get to your apps, tap "Gmail," and tap "Compose a New Email" (the little round red pencil in the lower right corner). When you're done, tap the send button.

You can also use the Google Play Store to find other email apps (such as Outlook).

MANAGE MULTIPLE EMAIL ACCOUNTS

If you have more than one Gmail account, tap the three lines at the upper left of your email screen; this brings out a slider menu. If you tap on the little arrow next to the email address, it drops down and will show other accounts. If none are listed, you can add one.

SURFING THE INTERNET

Google's native Web browser is Chrome. You can use other browsers (which can be found in the Google Play Store). This book will only cover Chrome, however.

Get started by tapping on the Chrome browser icon from your favorite bar, or by going into all programs.

If you've used Chrome on a desktop or any other device, then this chapter won't exactly be rocket science—just like the email app, many of the same properties you find on the desktop exist on the mobile version.

When you open it, you'll see it's a pretty basic browser. There are three main things that you'll want to note.

- **Address Bar** - As you would guess, this is where you put the Internet address you want to go to (google.com, for example); what you should understand, however is that this is not just an address bar. This is a search bar. You can use it to search for things just as you would searching for something on Google; when you hit the enter key, it takes you to the Google search results page.

- **Tab Button** - Because you are limited in space, you don't actually see all your tabs like you would on a normal browser; instead you get a button that tells you how many tabs are open. If you tap it, you can either toggle between the tabs, or swipe over one of the pages to close the tab.

- **Menu Button** - The last button brings up a menu with a series of other options that I'll talk about next.

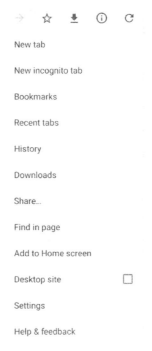

The menu is pretty straightforward, but there are a few things worth noting.

"New incognito tab" opens your phone into private browsing; that doesn't mean your IP isn't tracked. It means your history isn't record; it also means passwords and cookies aren't stored.

A little bit further down is "History"; if you want your history erased so there's no record on your phone of where you went, then go here, and clear your browsing history.

History ⓘ Q ✕

Your Google Account may have other forms of browsing history at myactivity.google.com.

CLEAR BROWSING DATA...

If you want to erase more than just websites (passwords, for example) then go to "Settings" at the very bottom of the menu. This opens up more advance settings.

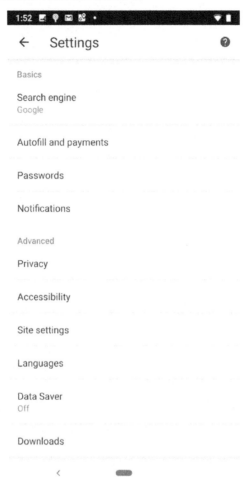

[6]
SNAP IT!

This chapter will cover:
- How to take different photos
- How to take videos
- Camera settings
- Different camera features

The camera is the bread and butter of the Moto G phone. So I'm sure you are eager to get started. Let's go!

THE BASICS

Are you ready to get your Ansel Adams on? Let's get started by opening the Camera app. You can do this several ways:
- The most obvious is to tap the Camera on your favorite bar or by swiping up and opening it from all apps. It looks like a camera—go figure!

Camera

- Double press the power button.

When you open the app, it starts in the basic camera mode. The UI can look pretty simple, but don't be fooled. There are a lot of controls.

The first is at the top. Tap the down arrow at the top of the screen.

The options are straightforward, but "Action Photos" might be new to you. This is basically like a very short video of your photo. You can turn it on for all photos, auto so it turns on when motion is detected, or turn it off. Motion is larger, so storing it in this mode will take a little more space. You can also press the config button in the lower corner to see even more options. The screen below is the basic camera settings, but this menu can differ slightly depending on what camera mode you are in.

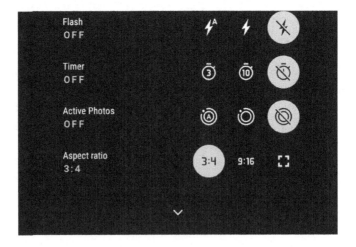

On the bottom of the screen are all the modes and the shutter. Starting with the top row from the left you have the selfie button, the shutter, and the last photo preview (tapping that will show all of your photos that you have taken starting with the most recent). On the bottom, you have the camera modes, which I'll cover in more detail later in this chapter.

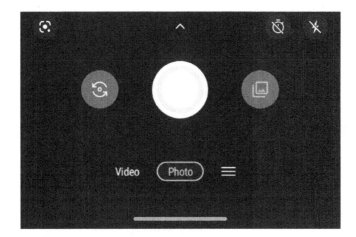

When you point your camera at a product and tap and hold over that product, this will activate Google Lens, which will try to detect what you are pointing at and give you more information about it. It's not always 100%.

If you tap once, but don't hold, this will bring up exposure and zoom options (you can also pinch in and out to zoom). Tapping on the area of the screen that you want to focus on will also focus on that area; for example, if you point it at a group of people in front of a crowd of people, you can tap the group to tell the camera that's the focus of the show.

The settings that pop up when you tap the screen are pretty easy to understand. The lock button will lock in the focus. The two sliders control the brightness and saturation. You could technically do these things after you take a photo as well. The bottom slider controls the zoom.

CAMERA MODES

Let's look at each of the modes next.

Think of modes like different lenses. You have your basic camera lens, but then you can also have a lens for fisheye, and close up. If you look at the bottom of your camera app, you can slide left and right to toggle between photo and video. But you'll also notices three lines to the right of Photos. That's where you'll find more camera options.

Depending on your phone (some phones might have a few extra modes), there's six photo modes and 1 video mode.

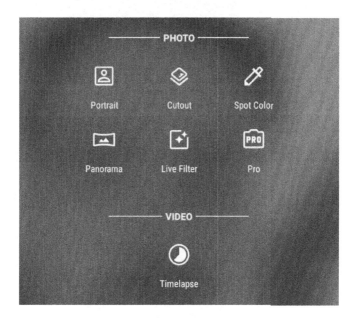

Video mode takes, you guessed it, videos! Once you tap record, there are not as many settings as the camera. To the left, there's a pause button, the middle is the stop button, and the far right is the camera shutter—that means as you are recording you can still take photos.

When you tap to focus on a subject, you'll notice that there's only a slider for zoom (bottom), and brightness (right side); there's also a lock to lock in on your focus.

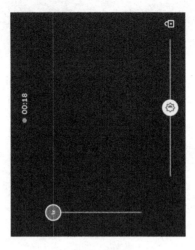

Before you shoot a video, there's also an option to toggle between Slow Motion, Normal, and Time Lapse.

EDITING PHOTO

Once you take a photo, you can begin fine tuning it to really make it sparkle. You can access editing by opening the photo you want to make edits to. This is done by either opening it from the camera app by clicking on the photo preview (next to the shutter);

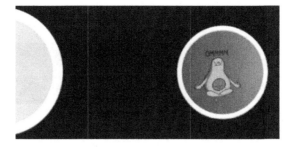

Or by opening the Photo app.

Photos

When you open a photo, you'll see either four or five sets of options depending on what kind of photo it is. Portrait photos have more editing options. How do you know what kind of photo it is? The thumbnail will tell you. If you see a timestamp, then it's a video; if there's nothing, then it's a regular photo; if there's a portrait, then it's a Portrait photo; and if there's a moon, then it was taken with Night mode.

The below are the four options available to all pictures.

And these five options are the ones available to only Portrait photos. Same options, but one additional new one. The middle option is new.

From left to right, the five buttons mean this:
- Share the photo
- Edit the photo
- Keep only one photo (Google takes several shots and will show you the best one)
- Turn on lens
- Delete the photo

The option you want is the second: edit the photo.

Tapping this brings up an option to change the saturation of the photo—you can slide to the right and see all the options.

On the bottom, you'll see a little control button: tap that.

This brings another set of options; the bottom option is Blur. That's what you want to change to edit the blur.

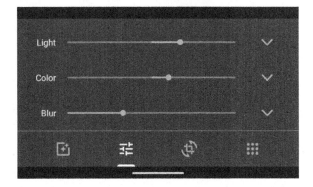

Note: Blur is only available on Portrait photos.

When you tap the Blur slider to adjust the intensity of the blur, you can also move the focal point. As an example, the picture below originally had Mickey as very sharp and everything else as blurred; I moved the focal point (the little circle in the photo) and now Mickey is more blurred.

You can edit the photo the same way you would the Portrait mode, but you'll notice depth is gone. In its place, it says "Pop." It makes the focal point stand out more, but does not have the same blur effect.

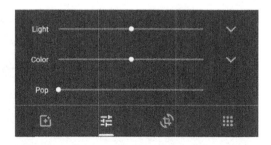

On the top of any photo you are editing there is a star and three dots. If you tap the star it will favorite a photo and show up in your album (covered in the next section). If you click the three dots, it will bring up an option menu.

One helpful editing option in this menu is "Edit in Markup."

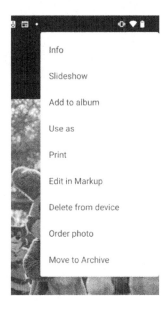

As the name implies, Edit in Markup lets you use a digital marker to draw or write on top of your photo.

ORGANIZING YOUR PHOTOS

The great thing about mobile photos is you always have a camera ready to capture memorable events; the bad thing about mobile photos is you always have a camera ready to capture events, and you'll find you have hundreds and hundreds of photos very quickly.

Fortunately, Google makes it very simple to organize your photos so you can find what you are looking for.

Let's open up the Photos app and see how to get things organized.

Photos

Moto G keeps things pretty simple by having only four options on the bottom of your screen.

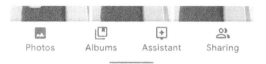

In the upper right corner, there's three dots, which is the photo option menu; that menu is there no matter where you are in the Photo app.

When you tap that menu, you'll get several more options.

The options are as follows:
- Select – This lets you select photos on your screen so you can share, email, print, and more.
- Layout – There are two Layout modes: Comfortable view (this view creates a grid with small and large photo thumbnails) and Month view (all thumbnails are the same size).

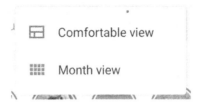

- Album – Let's you create an album by selecting photos or faces.

- Shared album – Lets you share albums.
- Prints – Quickly create photo albums that you can print and have sent to your house.

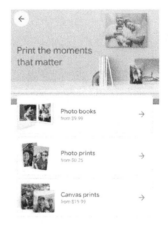

- Movie – Movies lets you create video memories of your photos. You can either select "New movie" and create one based on selected photos or pick from one of the many templates. It can take several minutes for movies to generate when you pick this option.

- Animation – Animation is kind of like a .gif; whereas movies could run for several minutes, animations are only a few seconds.
- Collage – Collage lets you pick up to nine photos to combine into one collage. If you pick less, Google will automatically arrange it for you. The below is an example of three photos in a collage. There isn't a lot of customization here, so if you want a collage, you might want to download a free collage app that has a few more tools in it.

In the upper left corner is three lines; this opens your second menu option screen.

Some of the options (such as buy prints) are the same ones you've already seen in the other menu.

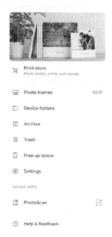

Photo frames is an option available if you have a Google Nest Hub (or Google Hub). This lets you pick the photos that display on your Hub.

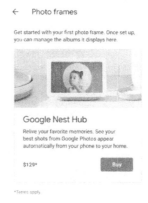

Device folders is where you can find screenshots if you've taken any. You can take a screenshot by pressing the orange button and the down volume button at the same time.

Archive is to help you declutter your phone. You can archive photos so your main photo area has less photos; archiving them puts them here, but they will still be searchable.

Clear the clutter

Archived items will be kept here. They'll still show in albums & search results.

Learn More

If you delete a photo, it is actually not permanently deleted from your device…yet. It is moved here. This is helpful if you have a kid who likes to delete things! If you tap any of the photos, you can restore it or delete it—deleting it means it's gone for good.

"Free up space" removes photos from your device and backs them up to your Google account. You can still view them whenever you want.

Settings will be covered in the next sections.

Finally, PhotoScan is a free app that you have to download to use; the app lets you use your Moto G camera to scan old print photos. It works surprisingly well and is recommended if you have lots of photos that you want saved.

The next tab on the bottom of the Photos app (Albums) is where you can go to start grouping your photos together. There are already things like Places and Things that have albums; if you have starred anything, you'll also see one for Favorites.

What you might not know is Google is quietly working in the background to figure out who is in photos. Once you take several photos, you'll see one called People & Pets.

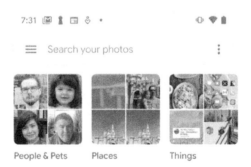

When you open it, you'll see people you probably recognize, and when you click on it, it will show you other photos that they are in. Pretty cool, right? What's cooler is you can name those people, so you can search more easily for them. Just click their face, then tap

"Add a name." In the example below, Google has found my dog's face.

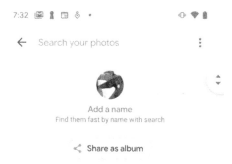

I added her name, so when I go back, I now see her photo with her name. I can now search for photos using her name. You can also search for photos using names of places or even foods or things. The photo search is pretty smart, and it gets even smarter as you take more photos.

When you want to create a new album, just click the three dots in the upper right corner.

It will ask you to name it; you can pick whatever you want. From here, you can either auto select things based on people and pets, or you can select your own photos.

If you select photos on your own, you'll just have to manually tap each one that you want in the album.

If you select to have it auto create, you'll just have to pick what you want to use (a person's name, for example).

Once the album is created, you can tap the three dots in the upper right corner to add more photos, order photos, delete the album, or share.

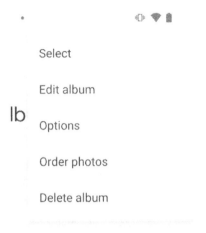

Select

Edit album

Options

Order photos

Delete album

You can also click the Share button on the album (or on any photo), which brings up the Sharing menu. You can share with a link, via email, Bluetooth, text message, and more.

The Assistant option is recommendations from Google's AI bot; it collects memories based on places you've been and groups together what it considers the best shots.

The last option on the bottom menu is Sharing. Sharing lets you select other people who can see your photos. You can, for example, share all photos of a certain person with that person, and you can set it to share new photos of that person whenever you take them.

To get started, just tap the "Add partner account."

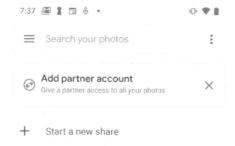

Next you'll see a screen telling you what sharing is. Tap the blue "Get Started" option.

From here you'll search for the person's name or email; Google might also have a few suggested contacts for you, and you can just tap their name.

Once you pick the person, it will ask you what you want to share. You can share every single photo now, and in the future, or you can pick certain people or days.

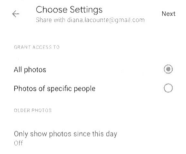

It will confirm what you are sharing before it shares; once you tap "Send invitation," it will email an invite to that person and they have to accept it before they actually see the photos.

SETTINGS

You probably won't spend a lot of time in Photo settings, but they're still good to know for those occasions when you do want to make changes.

You can access your settings by opening the Photo app, tapping on the three lines in the upper left corner, then tapping on Settings.

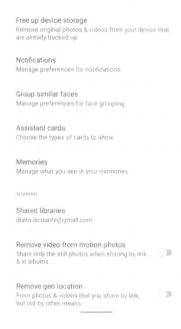

There are three areas of the settings: Main, Sharing, and Google apps.

MAIN SETTINGS

- Back up & sync – Lets you pick how photos are backed up (what email account they are linked to, the resolution of the photos, when to back them up, where to back them up, and more).
- Free up device storage – Removes photos from your device and stores them in your account so you have more room for additional photos.
- Notifications – Lets you pick the kinds of pop up notifications you'll receive regarding photos (suggested

sharing, printing promotions, photo book drafts, suggested photo books).

- Group similar faces – Turn on and off face grouping; if you don't want a robot scanning your photos to figure out the person that's in the shot, you can disable it here.
- Assistant cards – Picks the cards that show up in the Assistant menu of the Photos app (Creations, Rediscover this day, Recent highlights, Suggested Rotations, Suggested Archive).
- Memories – Memories are usually fun; seeing Google show you a photo of your kid as a baby can put a smile on your face as you start your day. But sometimes memories can suck—you go through a messy divorce or a loved one dies, and Google is there to remind you of their face. You can take those people out of your memories here. It doesn't delete them from your account; you just won't see them show up in your feed.

SHARING SETTINGS

- Shared libraries – Lets you see who can view your photos.
- Remove video from motion photos – Motion photos are nice—they're also big. If you prefer to just show the photo and not the video clip that goes with it, you can turn it off here.
- Remove geo location – Your photos have geo tags on them (unless you turn them off); that means when you share a photo, it might have things like your home address. If you don't want people to see that, then you can disable geo location with the people you are sharing it with.

GOOGLE APPS

- Google Location settings – Lets you pick what apps can see your photos.
- Google Lens – Not a setting as much as instructions about how to use the app.

[7]

GOING BEYOND

This chapter will cover:
* System settings

If you want to take total control of your Moto G, then you need to know where the system settings are and what can and can't be changed there.

First the easy part: the system settings are located with the rest of your apps. Swipe up, and scroll down to "Settings."

Settings

This opens all the settings available:
* Network & Internet
* Connected devices
* Apps & notification
* Battery
* Display

- Sound
- Storage
- Privacy
- Location
- Security
- Accounts
- Accessibility
- Digital Wellbeing
- Google
- About phone
- System
- Tips & support

I'll cover what each setting does in this chapter.

NETWORK & INTERNET

This setting, like most settings, does exactly what it sounds like: connects to the Internet. If you need to connect to a new wireless connection (or disconnect from one) you can do it here. Tapping on the current wireless lets you see other networks, and the toggle lets you switch it on and off.

Mobile network is for your carrier (Verizon, AT&T, Sprint, etc.).

Data usage tells you how much data you've used; tapping on it gives you a deeper overview, so you can see exactly which apps used the data. Why is this important? For most, it probably won't be. I'll give an example of when it helped me: I work on the go a lot; I use the wireless on my phone to connect my laptop (which is called tethering); my MacBook was set to back-up to the cloud, and little did I know it was doing this while connecting to my phone...20GB later, I was able to pinpoint what happened by looking at the data.

Below this is Hotspot & tethering. This is when you use your phone's data to connect other devices; you can use your phone's data plan, for example, to use the Internet on your iPad. Some carriers charge extra for this—mine (AT&T) includes it in the plan. To use it, tap the setting and turn it on, then name your network and password. From your other device, you find the network you set up, and connect.

Airplane mode is next. This setting turns off all wireless activity with a switch. So if your flying and they tell you to turn everything wireless of, you can do it with a switch.

Finally, Advanced is for doing some wireless connecting on a private network. This is not something a beginning user would need to do, and I'm not going to cover it, as the point of this book is to keep it ridiculously simple.

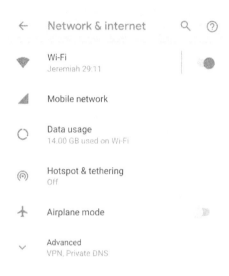

CONNECTED DEVICES

"Connected devices" is Google's way of saying Bluetooth. If you have something that connects via Bluetooth (such as a car radio or headphones) then tap "Pair new device." If you've previously paired something, then it will show below and you can simply tap it to reconnect.

←   Connected devices   🔍   ⑦

\+   Pair new device

🔲   Previously connected devices

       Connection preferences
       Bluetooth, driving mode, NFC

ⓘ   Visible as "Pixel 3" to other devices

APPS & NOTIFICATION

Every app you download has different settings and permissions. A map app, for example, needs your permission to know your location. You can turn these permissions on and off here. Does it really matter? App makers can't abuse it, right? Sort of. Here's an example: a few months ago, a popular ride-sharing app made headlines because it wanted to know where passengers were after they left the ride, so they could promote different restaurants and stores and make even more money. Many felt this was both greedy and an invasion of privacy; if you are of the latter stance, then you could go in here and stop sharing your location.

How? Just tap "Advanced" then look at all the permissions you are giving away. Go to the permission you are concerned with and toggle the app from on to off.

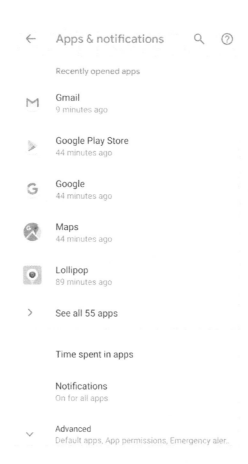

BATTERY

The battery setting is more about analytics than settings you can change. There are some settings here you can edit—you can put your phone in battery saving mode, for example. This setting is more useful if your battery is draining too quickly; it helps you troubleshoot what's going on so you can get more life from your phone.

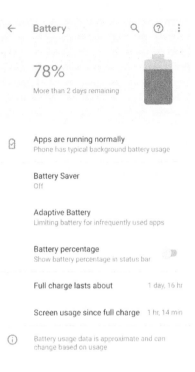

← Battery   🔍   ⊙   ⋮

78%
More than 2 days remaining

Apps are running normally
Phone has typical background battery usage

Battery Saver
Off

Adaptive Battery
Limiting battery for infrequently used apps

Battery percentage
Show battery percentage in status bar

Full charge lasts about   1 day, 16 hr

Screen usage since full charge   1 hr, 14 min

ⓘ   Battery usage data is approximate and can change based on usage

DISPLAY

As with most of the settings, almost all the main features of the Display setting can be changed outside of the app. If you tap "Advanced," however, you'll see some settings not in other places. These include changing colors and font sizes.

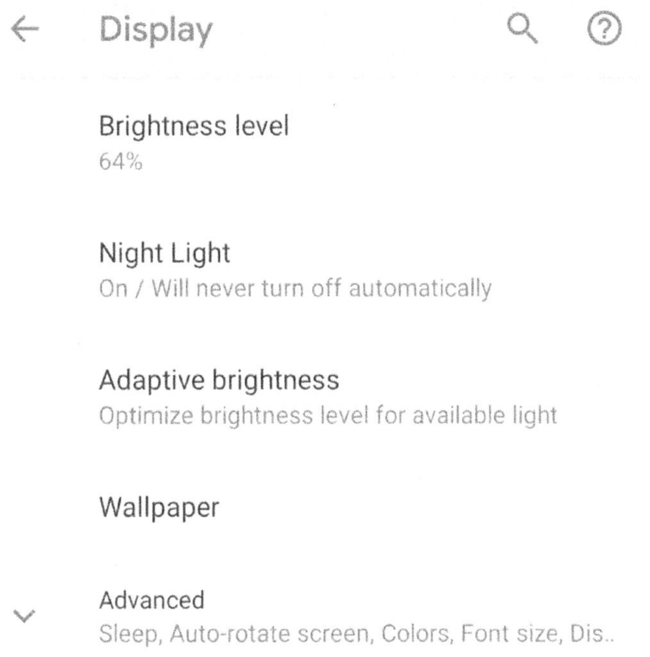

Brightness level
64%

Night Light
On / Will never turn off automatically

Adaptive brightness
Optimize brightness level for available light

Wallpaper

⌄   Advanced
Sleep, Auto-rotate screen, Colors, Font size, Dis..

SOUND

There's a volume button on the side of your phone, so why would you need to open up a setting for it?! This setting lets you get more specific about your volume.

For example, you may want your alarm to ring super loud in the morning, but you want your music to play very low.

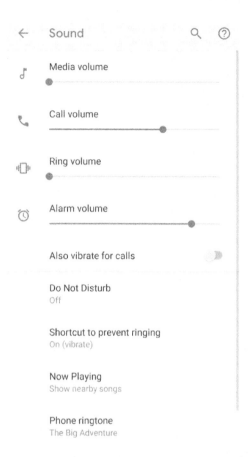

STORAGE

When you first get your phone, storage won't be a big issue, but once you start taking photos (which are larger than you think) and installing apps, it's going to go very quickly.

The storage setting helps you manage this. It shows you what's taking up storage, so you can decide if you want to delete things. Just tap on any of the subsections and follow the instructions for what to do to save space.

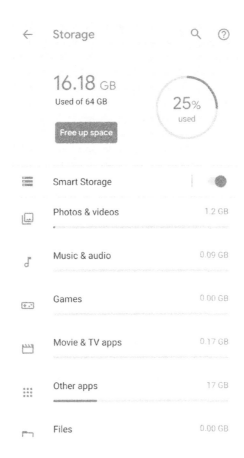

PRIVACY

Like Location Control (covered below), Privacy settings got a big upgrade in Android 11. It's so big, it now fills an entire section in the settings.

Go to System > Privacy and tap "Advanced" to see all of them.

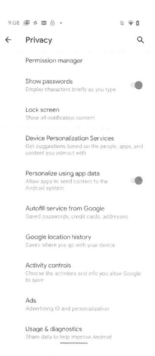

The biggest upgrade is the ability to customize what apps see what; it's no longer all or nothing. You can refine exactly how much or how little each app can see.

Tap on "Permissions" as one example of what you can control.

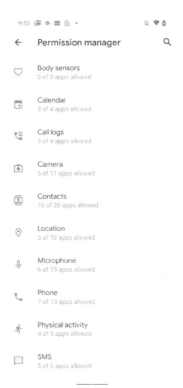

LOCATION

In the past, Location Control was an all or nothing feature—you'd decide if an app could see you all the time or none of the time. That's nice for privacy, but not nice for when you actually need someone to know your location—like when you are getting picked up by a ride app like Lyft. The new Android OS adds a new option for while you are using the app. So, for example, a ride app can only see your location while you are using the app; once the ride is over, they can no longer see what you are doing.

To pick what location an app can see, go to System > Location and select the app, then tap when they can see your location.

Google Play Store

LOCATION ACCESS FOR THIS APP

○ **Allow all the time**

○ **Allow only while using the app**

◉ **Deny**

SECURITY & LOCATION

If you want to change your lock screen, add an additional fingerprint, or turn on / off the find your phone setting, you can do it here.

Security status

Google Play Protect
Apps scanned at 9:03 AM

Find My Device
On

Security update
September 5, 2018

Device security

Screen lock
PIN   ⚙

ACCOUNTS

If you have more than one Google account, you can tap on this to add it. If you want to remove your current account, tap on it and tap remove—remember, however, you can have more than one account. Don't remove it just so you can add another.

ACCESSIBILITY

Do you hate phones because the text is too small, the colors are all wrong, you can't hear anything? Or something else? That's where accessibility can help. This is where you make changes to the device to make it easier on your eyes or ears.

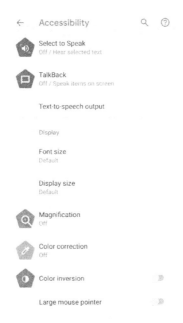

DIGITAL WELLBEING

Digital Wellbeing is my least favorite feature on the Moto G phone; now when my wife says "You spend too much time on your phone"—she can actually prove it! The purpose of the setting is to help you manage your time more. It lets you know your spending 12 hours a day updating your social media with memes of cats, and "hopefully" make you feel like perhaps you shouldn't do that.

The setting is in beta and isn't perfect. You can see in the example below, for example, that I spent nearly 8 hours in an app called Lollipop. What a time-waster, right? While I technically did spend that much time in the app, what it doesn't show is that Lollipop is a baby monitor and the reason it's so high is that it was on all night.

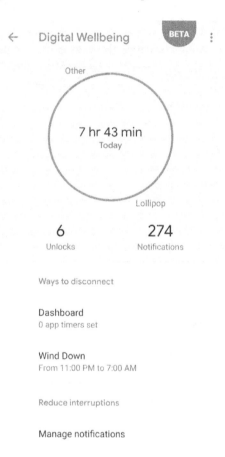

GOOGLE

Google is where you will go to manage any Google device connected with your phone. If you are using a Google watch, for example; or a Chromecast.

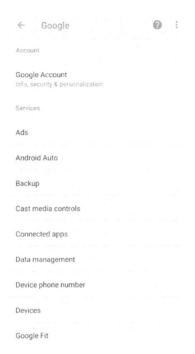

← Google   ❓ ⋮

Account

Google Account
Info, security & personalization

Services

Ads

Android Auto

Backup

Cast media controls

Connected apps

Data management

Device phone number

Devices

Google Fit

SYSTEM UPDATE

System is important for one very important reason: system updates. If you don't have your phone set to download updates automatically, then you'll have to do it manually here.

ABOUT PHONE

This is where you will find general information about your phone. Such as the OS you are running, the kind of phone you have, IP address, etc. It's more of an FYI, but there are a few settings here that you can change.

INDEX

ABOUT THE AUTHOR

Scott La Counte is a librarian and writer. His first book, *Queit, Please: Dispatches from a Public Librarian* (Da Capo 2008) was the editor's choice for the Chicago Tribune and a Discovery title for the Los Angeles Times; in 2011, he published the YA book The N00b Warriors, which became a #1 Amazon bestseller; his most recent book is *#OrganicJesus: Finding Your Way to an Unprocessed, GMO-Free Christianity* (Kregel 2016).

He has written dozens of best-selling how-to guides on tech products.

You can connect with him at ScottDouglas.org.

Made in the USA
Monee, IL
14 February 2023

27850194R00075